*Greater
available in Ebook and Audiobook format.

Greater Than a Tourist Book Series
Reviews from Readers

I think the series is wonderful and beneficial for tourists to get information before visiting the city.

-Seckin Zumbul, Izmir Turkey

I am a world traveler who has read many trip guides but this one really made a difference for me. I would call it a heartfelt creation of a local guide expert instead of just a guide.

-Susy, Isla Holbox, Mexico

New to the area like me, this is a must have!

-Joe, Bloomington, USA

This is a good series that gets down to it when looking for things to do at your destination without having to read a novel for just a few ideas.

-Rachel, Monterey, USA

Good information to have to plan my trip to this destination.

-Pennie Farrell, Mexico

Great ideas for a port day.
-Mary Martin USA

Aptly titled, you won't just be a tourist after reading this book. You'll be greater than a tourist!
-Alan Warner, Grand Rapids, USA

Even though I only have three days to spend in San Miguel in an upcoming visit, I will use the author's suggestions to guide some of my time there. An easy read - with chapters named to guide me in directions I want to go.
-Robert Catapano, USA

Great insights from a local perspective! Useful information and a very good value!
-Sarah, USA

This series provides an in-depth experience through the eyes of a local. Reading these series will help you to travel the city in with confidence and it'll make your journey a unique one.
-Andrew Teoh, Ipoh, Malaysia

GREATER THAN A TOURIST- ST. LOUIS MISSOURI USA

50 Travel Tips from a Local

Jessica London

Cover designed by: Ivana Stamenkovic
Cover Image: https://pixabay.com/photos/arch-spring-saint-louis-usa-garden-712470/

CZYK Publishing Since 2011.

Greater Than a Tourist

Lock Haven, PA
All rights reserved.

ISBN: 9781706213130

>TOURIST

50 TRAVEL TIPS FROM A LOCAL

BOOK DESCRIPTION

Are you excited about planning your next trip? Do you want to try something new? Would you like some guidance from a local? If you answered yes to any of these questions, then this Greater Than a Tourist book is for you. Greater Than a Tourist- St. Louis, Missouri, United States by Jessica London offers the inside scoop on Missouri. Most travel books tell you how to travel like a tourist. Although there is nothing wrong with that, as part of the Greater Than a Tourist series, this book will give you travel tips from someone who has lived at your next travel destination.

In these pages, you will discover advice that will help you throughout your stay. This book will not tell you exact addresses or store hours but instead will give you excitement and knowledge from a local that you may not find in other smaller print travel books.

Travel like a local. Slow down, stay in one place, and get to know the people and culture. By the time you finish this book, you will be eager and prepared to travel to your next destination.

Inside this travel guide book you will find:

- Insider tips from a local.

- Packing and planning list.

- List of travel questions to ask yourself or others while traveling.

- A place to write your travel bucket list.

OUR STORY

Traveling is a passion of the Greater than a Tourist book series creator. Lisa studied abroad in college, and for their honeymoon Lisa and her husband toured Europe. During her travels to Malta, an older man tried to give her some advice based on his own experience living on the island since he was a young boy. She was not sure if she should talk to the stranger but was interested in his advice. When traveling to some places she was wary to talk to locals because she was afraid that they weren't being genuine. Through her travels, Lisa learned how much locals had to share with tourists. Lisa created the Greater Than a Tourist book series to help connect people with locals. A topic that locals are very passionate about sharing.

TABLE OF CONTENTS

13. Imagine the impossible at The Magic House

14. Apple Picking / Pumpkin Patch

15. Hollywood Wax Museum Entertainment Center

16. Climb up an Airplane at the City Museum

An Animal Lovers Paradise

17. Get face-to-face with a Polar Bear at St. Louis
     Zoo

18. Experience a Butterfly Zoo

19. Endangered Wolf Center

20. Saint Louis Aquarium at Union Station

Festivals and Celebrations

21. Big Muddy Blues Festival

22. Party the day away at St. Louis Mardi Gras

23. Art Fair at Laumeier Sculpture Park

24. Feel the love at Pride Fest

25. Go international at Festival of Nations

Live Theater Shows

26. The Municipal Theatre Association (The Muny)

27. Catch a show at Fox Theatre

28. Burlesque at the Boom Boom Room

Sports Fanatics

29. Be a part of Cardinal Nation

30. Stanley Cup winning Blues

31. Tailgate in red with the Kansas City Chiefs

32. Wear some boots and head to the Rodeo

Music and Nightlife

DEDICATION

This book is dedicated to my beautiful mother. You are and have always been my biggest supporter. You are the essence of strength and a constant source of inspiration.

ABOUT THE AUTHOR

Jessica London is a writer and English tutor who lives in St. Louis, MO. She loves to travel and explore hidden gems all over the world, including in her home state. She was born and raised in Missouri with her family and friends. Through her travels abroad she has come to realize why home is so special, and all that it truly has to offer. Here are 50 tips from the perspective of a locally born tourist.

HOW TO USE THIS BOOK

The *Greater Than a Tourist* book series was written by someone who has lived in an area for over three months. The goal of this book is to help travelers either dream or experience different locations by providing opinions from a local. The author has made suggestions based on their own experiences. Please check before traveling to the area in case the suggested places are unavailable.

Travel Advisories: As a first step in planning any trip abroad, check the Travel Advisories for your intended destination.
https://travel.state.gov/content/travel/en/traveladvisories/traveladvisories.html

FROM THE PUBLISHER

Traveling can be one of the most important parts of a person's life. The anticipation and memories that you have are some of the best. As a publisher of the Greater Than a Tourist, as well as the popular *50 Things to Know* book series, we strive to help you learn about new places, spark your imagination, and inspire you. Wherever you are and whatever you do I wish you safe, fun, and inspiring travel.

Lisa Rusczyk Ed. D.
CZYK Publishing

WELCOME TO
> TOURIST

*"There'll be the lightning bugs
with their Morse code on display,
And shooting stars and
constellations to befriend; The
dragonflies will keep us from going
astray, As we search for new
adventures 'round every bend."*

– Mariecor Ruediger

Looking for beer, baseball, and pizza? Missouri is the place for you! The "Show-Me" state is brimming with amazing and unique experiences that cater to every season. No matter if you're interests are outdoors, sports, music, family fun, or food, I've got you covered!

St. Louis
Missouri, USA

St. Louis Climate

	High	Low
January	40	23
February	45	27
March	56	38
April	67	48
May	77	58
June	86	67
July	90	71
August	88	69
September	81	61
October	70	50
November	57	39
December	44	29

GreaterThanaTourist.com

Temperatures are in Fahrenheit degrees.
Source: NOAA

13

FOODIE ON A MISSION

*"Food is everything we are. It's
an extension of nationalist feeling,
ethnic feeling, your personal
history, your province, your region,
your tribe, your grandma. It's
inseparable from those from the
get-go."*

– Anthony Bourdain

1. ENJOY TOP NOTCH BBQ

Missourians know good barbeque, and we love to
prove it by hosting competitions all year long. No
matter the time of the year, you're likely to find some
sort of festival centered on smoked meats. Among the
top dives in Saint Louis are Pappy's Smokehouse,
Salt + Smoke, and Sugarfire Smokehouse (my
personal favorite). If you're in Kansas City (where's
claimed to have the best in the country) stop by A
Little BBQ Joint, Q39-Midtown, and Arthur Bryant's
Barbeque. Word to the wise - bring a bib, some wet
wipes, and your stretchy pants.

Bonus – We've also got some pretty tasty, albeit spicy barbeque chips. If you like a little extra kick, try our infamous Old Vienna Red Hot Riplets, which can be found at almost any nearby grocery stores.

2. PIZZA WITH TOASTED RAVIOLIS

As a thin-crust loving girl, I'm a little biased in saying that Imo's pizza is my favorite. Imo's pizza has been a staple in Missouri homes for over 50 years, and is usually the first slice we grab on game days. But if thin isn't your style, no worries. Ask for an order of toasted raviolis with red sauce! Warning: regular raviolis will never be the same. Other local favorites include Dewey's, Shakespeare's, and Stefanina's.

3. SAMPLE LOCAL ICE CREAM

Frtiz's, Ted Drewes, Andy's, Kilwins, take your pick. Missourians love our ice cream and supporting local businesses. Did you know that St. Louis, Missouri is famed for being the location of the first ice cream phone? The folklore tale states that the World Fair of 1904 hosted in our city is the first spot this frosty treat came into creation. Many families have been going to the same location for generations. Grab a scoop and watch the sunset on a warm summer night for the perfect ending to your day of adventure.

Bonus – Not to be left out of our sweet treat originals is the renowned Gooey Butter Cake. Residents in Missouri know it as a staple in our homes. (My mom's is the best though!)

4. GET LOST IN SOULARD FARMER'S MARKET

Come visit the oldest operating public market west of the Mississippi River. It's a half-mile from Anheuser Busch and is teeming with stalls of local fresh fruits, veggies, meats, cheeses, spices, flowers, and yummy baked goods. The market is only open Wednesday through Saturday. I recommend going in the early morning as some vendors run out of best sellers a bit early or begin to pack up when it slows down. Check out their website for a map of vendors and events!

If it gets too crowded, take a breather and explore the surrounding Soulard neighborhood. It offers a collection of restaurants, bars, and shops that are popular with locals. I recommend a visit to Molly's in Soulard, Mission Taco Joint, or John D. McGurk's Irish Pub, or Clementine's Naught & Nice Creamery for some yummy food and drinks!

5. ITALIAN HAVEN THE HILL

If you've been searching for the premier spot for delicious Italian food, look no further. St. Louis's version of little Italy is bursting with great restaurants and shops owned by locals. You'll know when you've entered the neighborhood as colors of green, white, and red begin appearing on flagpoles, fire hydrants, and street lights in a nod to Italian pride. Arrive hungry and visit some top favorites including Missouri Baking Company, Mama's on The Hill, Charlie Gitto's on the Hill (a bit pricier), and Zia's Restaurant.

THE OUTDOOR ENTHUSIAST

"Wilderness is not a luxury but necessity of the human spirit."

– Edward Abbey

6. MOUNTAIN BIKE / HIKE AT CASTLEWOOD STATE PARK

This is for those travelers that love the smell of fresh air and getting their blood pumping on their adventures! Take in the beautiful views of the Meramec River or catch a glimpse of local wildlife in the surrounding forest. There are also options for fishing, kayaking, picnics, and new playgrounds to monkey around on. Some of the more popular trails for hiking and biking include River Scene Trail Loop (medium difficulty), Lone Wolf Trail (medium difficulty), Grotpeter Trail (medium difficulty), and Castlewood Trail (easy). I recommend downloading an app such as AllTrails for detailed maps and descriptions. I recommend going during weekdays to avoid the crowds.

7. EXPLORE MERAMEC CAVERNS

This pristine 400 million year-old cavern is rich in history and lore. It offers tours regularly and prices are relatively cheap. Tours usually take around an hour and a half and you'll cover a little over a mile in distance. Keep an eye out for various species of bats that call these caves home, infrequent sightings do occur but don't worry, they're harmless! Temperatures in the cave hover around 58 degrees Fahrenheit so be sure to dress in layers and wear comfortable shoes. Reservations aren't necessary (unless you have a big group) and bathrooms won't be available inside so use them before you begin! Have fun exploring the same caves that indigenous peoples were recorded traversing as far back as the 1700's!

8. ELEPHANT ROCKS STATE PARK

While I can't promise you'll find elephants at this state owned park, I can promise you'll find a great day outdoor activities! Located about an hour and a half south of St. Louis you'll find a naturally made amusement park of sorts. Beautiful granite rocks that have eroded over time give the appearance of elephants huddled together in colors of pink, white, and tan. There are hiking paths you can take (handicap accessible) to explore these formations, or you can simply forge your own and explore with freedom.

The main attraction here is the fun you get as you climb, leap, and hop your way from place to place. Many people can spend 3 hours or more here, so I recommend grabbing some food along your drive and making an afternoon of it. There are bathrooms available for use and sometimes water fountains (occasionally they are shut off). Stock up on a few water bottles and wear some comfortable shoes for a day of climbing massive rocks and maybe even an adrenaline rush. The boulder climbing and jumping is something to take at your own pace and there are difficulty levels to match everyone's capabilities. This is an activity that is just as welcome for families with young children as it is for adults who enjoy free climbing.

9. SMELL THE ROSES AT MISSOURI BOTANICAL GARDENS

There's a reason why our gardens have over 8,000 positive reviews. These botanical gardens span across 79 acres and are home to a wide array of categorized conservatories and collections. Visit their website if you have a sought after favorite you want to locate. Some of the gardens most popular annual events include the Whitaker Music Festival (June-August), Japanese Festival (Labor Day weekend), and Garden Glow (November-December). Don't forget to visit the delicate and unique Flowering Dogwoods, our state tree. Bonus – if you're lucky enough to here during Arbor Day Giveaway, swing in and grab a free tree sapling!

10. REACH THE TOP OF MISSOURI AT TAUM SAUK

Taum Sauk Mountain State Park is known as having the highest "mountain" in Missouri. Those with an affliction for more rigorous trails will have a ball. Bring your hiking boots because while most trails here aren't extremely lengthy, the rocky terrain can be a challenge for many. Download a trail app such as AllTrails to ensure you don't miss your turns as some points tend to be not well marked deeper into the hike. Mina Sauk Falls trail is moderate difficulty and highly recommended as it leads you to Missouri's highest waterfall. Primitive camping is available as are campsites with more amenities. Maintained campground spots are cheap and cash only.

Close by Taum Sauk you'll find the Bell Mountain Wilderness and Trail. Located within the St. Francois Mountains, this rugged area is an excellent spot for backpacking, primitive camping, and hiking. The loop trail is about 12 miles in total and is best done over a two-day period. Hike up to the top of the mountain with your camping gear in tow and be sure to bring plenty of water / food / toilet paper as there are no facilities or amenities available on the trail or at the top. When you've reached the mountain's head, enjoy the gorgeous sunset views and build your fire above a night sky so unpolluted with city lights that you won't want to tear your eyes away. The second half of the journey down is a bit shorter and easier as it is mostly downhill. The trail and mountaintop is not as frequented as some easier trails in Missouri, so enjoy your solitude, peace, and the sounds of nature. Some parts of the trail can be quite exposed so bring your sunscreen if you burn easily!

11. SWIM AND CLIMB AT JOHNSON SHUT-INS

Splash and play with the whole family in this natural water park of wonder. Johnson Shut-ins is actually a state park but the main attraction has to be the geological anomaly that a fork in the Black River has created over so many years. Cell phone service is minimal here but there's a visitors center for those looking to inquire about maps, directions, or park amenities. Bring or buy water shoes with you because the large boulders and rocks have moss / algae and tend to get very slippery.

There are calmer areas for small kids to swim and play as well as larger, more active streams for the adults that want to do some climbing and exploring in the waters. Restrooms / showers are available for use as well as lockers to hold your belongings (for a fee). If you don't want to rent a locker you can always find a large boulder to lay your towel and clothes as many locals do. Seasonal camping is also a fun option for those that want to spend more time in this beautiful park. Make a reservation in advance as spots can go pretty quickly.

FAMILY FRIENDLY FUN

"Travelling in the company of those we love is home in motion."

– Leigh Hunt

12. GET NERDY AT ST. LOUIS SCIENCE CENTER

Relive your childhood here as you crane your neck to gawk at ceiling high dinosaurs, or have your brain waves put to the test in a mind relaxing competition. The St. Louis Science Center is especially suited for families and children. I recommend going during weekdays to avoid long lines, as they can accumulate quickly at the more popular attractions. Top attractions here include the McDonnell Planetarium, Omnimax Theater, and dinosaur exhibit. Be on the look out because occasionally the center will create a temporary themed installation that is sure to wow. Their most recent project brings to life the eruptions of ancient Pompeii!

Bonus – Less than two miles away you'll find the Central West End neighborhood. The streets of CWE are lined with upscale restaurants and shopping that aim to please. For the hungry patrons I recommend Bar Italia Ristorante or Dressel's Public House.

13. IMAGINE THE IMPOSSIBLE AT THE MAGIC HOUSE

The Magic House is the perfect place to take the kiddos to burn off excess energy and let their imaginations run wild! Growing up, my sister and I absolutely adored this nonprofit children's museum. Prices are very reasonable and re-entry is allowed! Plan to spend around 2 to 4 hours enjoying all the interactive exhibits the museum has to offer. Food is available for purchase inside as well. Be sure to snap a hilarious picture at the local favorite, the electrically charged ball that makes your hair stand up on contact.

The kids still wired from those cookies at lunch?
No problem! I have the perfect solution: Grant's
Farm. About 15 minutes away is a petting zoo
paradise. Admission and tram rides are free, but
parking and animal feed is not.

14. APPLE PICKING /
PUMPKIN PATCH

As you may already know, the Midwest is chocked
full of local farms. It's difficult to drive more than 10
miles without running into one, and as a result we
have come up with inventive ways to have some fun
with them. Apple and pumpkin picking is a great fall
activity that many visitors and locals enjoy as an
alternative to the usual supermarket outing. It's a
cheap way to get an inside look on where your food is
coming from, and leaves you with a sense of
accomplishment when you take home your hand
picked goodies. For apples, I recommend Herman's
Farm, Centennial Farms, or Thierbach Orchards &
Berry Farm. For pumpkins, check out Stuckmeyer's
Farm Market, Brookdale Farms, Inc., or Fun Farm
Pumpkin Patch.

15. HOLLYWOOD WAX MUSEUM ENTERTAINMENT CENTER

Are you feeling like doing something off the beaten path? Branson, Missouri has the answer for you. Go check out life size replicas of iconic movie stars and characters from your childhood in the wax museum. Next door you'll find an interactive mirror maze, mini golf, and 5D castle adventure. Buy an all access pass for a whole day of fun or a ticket for one if you have limited time. Check their website for hours because they change depending on the season.

Bonus – If you're looking for extra must sees in Branson, head over to the Branson Titanic Museum. They've got an incredible amount of artifacts on display and historical tours for those interested in gaining more insight on the tragedy that captured hearts around the world.

16. CLIMB UP AN AIRPLANE AT THE CITY MUSEUM

Ask anyone in St. Louis where he or she thinks the most unique and show-stopping place in this city is and they will tell you the City Museum. This place is more of an imaginative and interactive fun park for all ages. Creative architecture and thrills are around located in every square inch of this massive museum. From the roof, which boasts a climbing adventure that apex's to a gutted airplane, to the incredible 10-story slide, the childhood wonder in everyone comes alive here. Check their Facebook page, as they will sometimes host evening rooftop events with adult beverages and live music.

AN ANIMAL LOVERS PARADISE

"Until one has loved an animal,
a part of one's soul remains
unawakened."

– Anatole France

17. GET FACE-TO-FACE WITH A POLAR BEAR AT ST. LOUIS ZOO

Come see why St. Louis Zoo is consistently ranked as one of the top zoos in the USA. The new McDonnell Polar Bear Exhibit is one of the most popular attractions and currently homes our resident bear Kali. You can easily spend the day here so plan ample time to walk the large, and free, expanse of exhibits (and wear comfortable shoes!). Visit their website early if you're interested in booking an exclusive close-up experience because they require reservations to be make three weeks in advance. For most up close encounters the zoo also recommends children be at least 8 years old and you are required to wear close-toed shoes. Our zoo regularly hosts

31

themed evening events so that visitors can experience the wildlife after dark! For those visiting in the winter, fear not! It's also open year round (other than the week of Christmas / New Year's).

18. EXPERIENCE A BUTTERFLY ZOO

Owned and operated by the Missouri Botanical Gardens, the Sophia M. Sachs Butterfly House is located in Chesterfield, Missouri and hosts over 40 species of these elegant, winged creatures. The main attraction is the ornately designed conservatory that leads you on a path lined with gorgeous exotic flowers. It can get quite humid, so wear layered clothes that you can easily shed. Also dress in brightly colored clothes if you want to attract more butterflies to you! They often host interactive activities for children and have an array of bug exhibits if the creepy-crawlies are what pique your interest!

19. ENDANGERED WOLF CENTER

The goal of this conservation center is to help these beautiful creatures live happy lives in their natural environment with many being released into the wild. The center has many outstanding accolades to recognize their work in helping repopulate wolf species, in particular breeds such as the Mexican and red wolf. The facility is located just outside of St. Louis city and offers a wide variety of activities depending on what you're looking for. Tours, camp outs, children's programs, and even yoga events are all offered here. Book online or on the phone to reserve a spot, and do be mindful that some more exclusive tours can be on the pricier side.

20. SAINT LOUIS AQUARIUM AT UNION STATION

This underwater adventure is a new addition to the historic Union Station in downtown Saint Louis. The city decided to do away with an old mall that was no longer sustainable and turn it into an exciting project to spread awareness, knowledge, and fun to visitors. Outside food and drink isn't allowed in the facility but there are several dining options available inside. Take a tour or browse the 44 exhibits on your own that house over 250 species of animals.

Bonus – Union Station is an attraction of it's own and offers so many activities that you'll likely be able to spend the entire day here. From carousel rides, to mini golf, a St. Louis Ferris wheel ride, and a rope course, the possibilities are endless!

FESTIVALS AND CELEBRATIONS

*"Festivals promote diversity,
they bring neighbors into dialogue,
they increase creativity, they offer
opportunities for civic pride, they
improve our general psychological
well-being. In short, they make
cities better places to live."*

– David Binder

21. BIG MUDDY BLUES FESTIVAL

For over 20 years St. Louis has shown its appreciation for its soulful blues roots with the Big Muddy Fest. The festival is hosted on Labor Day weekend in Laclede's Landing and can see more than 20,000 people over the course of the weekend. Do keep in mind that items such as coolers, backpacks, large purses, bottles, and cans are not permitted. You'll be doing a decent amount of walking between stages and vendors so wear comfortable shoes / clothing (also keep in mind it can get very HOT in St.

Louis this time of year). Bonus – the newly opened National Blues Museum is a short walk away if you have time and want to learn more about the history of blues in the city.

22. PARTY THE DAY AWAY AT ST. LOUIS MARDI GRAS

Listed as one of the biggest celebrations in the country, this day of partying will not disappoint. Park your car and take the MetroLink or one of the many shuttles available to experience it in full. Be sure to wear warm clothes because temperatures outside can get bitterly cold. Stock up on alcohol/food in your bag to save money and arrive early as most locals begin the party as early as 9am.

If you've got the extra cash and aren't too keen on the cold I would also recommend buying a tent pass. Tents are great to escape the outside mayhem and get some shelter from the harsh winds. But they can get pricey and sell out fast so buy tickets online in advance. The Monster Tent, Bud Light Party Tent, and Blues Alumni Tent are always big and aim to give you some bang for your buck.

23. ART FAIR AT LAUMEIER SCULPTURE PARK

Have you ever seen an eyeball twice your height? Grab your camera and take some Instagram worthy pictures in this strange and beautiful sculpture park. The art installations can be followed along a pathway and even expands into the surrounding forest. The park hosts an annual art fair on Mother's Day weekend, which draws local vendors and their unique pieces from all over the state. The perfect place to find your one-of-a-kind souvenir!

24. FEEL THE LOVE AT PRIDE FEST

Come see the award winning celebration that has united St. Louis city for years. With numbers exceeding over 300,000 attendees throughout the weekend celebration, it is truly a sight to witness. The love and support that people in this city show for each other is especially beautiful to witness here. Donations of $5 are recommended for those that can give, but the event is free to everyone. This event is open to everyone and typically takes place in June.

Bathrooms, ATMs, and food vendors will all be available in plenty, as well as great performances for you to get your boogie on. Leave the tents, glass containers, outside alcohol, and coolers at home, and have a great time! The city can get very hot during this time of year so dress for the heat and bring sunscreen.

25. GO INTERNATIONAL AT FESTIVAL OF NATIONS

We love our food, and we love free events! Join Festival of Nations and get your fill of international cuisine while learning about cultures you might not otherwise have been exposed to. The event is held in Tower Grove Park in downtown St. Louis and is usually scheduled in late August. Several shuttle options are available for those that prefer it and car parking is also an option both inside and outside the park grounds. Activities for the whole family are plentiful and in the past we have had cultural dance lessons, religious Q & A, and world sports interactive demonstrations if you're up for the challenge!

LIVE THEATER SHOWS

"Great theater is about challenging how we think and encouraging us to fantasize about a world we aspire to."

– Willem Dafoe

26. THE MUNICIPAL THEATRE ASSOCIATION (THE MUNY)

The Municipal Theatre Association, otherwise known as The Muny, proudly boasts to be the largest and oldest outdoor theater in America. Stars of present and past such as Irene Dunne, Cary Grant, June Havoc, and Bob Hope have graced the Muny with their performances. This outdoor arena located inside Forest Park has been performing for audiences for over 100 years. They do provide shuttle and bus options, as well as dinner options (if you want to eat at the Culver Pavilion make reservations in advance). Don't forget to turn off your cell phones / put away your cameras during the performance. Dress casual and enjoy the show!

27. CATCH A SHOW AT FOX THEATRE

Otherwise known as the Fabulous Fox, this movie palace-turned-performance venue is gorgeous. Shows go on all year long regardless of inclement weather. Attire depends on the type of show, and can vary from business casual to evening dress / suit and tie. If you're really interested in snapping some pictures, check the policy ahead of time to ensure your camera is permitted in the theater. Food and drink are available for purchase inside the theater (and can be on the pricier side) so I recommend eating a nice meal before your show. The lobby opens one hour before show time, so don't get there too early or you may be waiting outside for a while.

28. BURLESQUE AT THE BOOM BOOM ROOM

Interested in something a bit more risqué? Reserve a few spots at an evening show in the Boom Boom Room. Yes, a burlesque show may be a bit outside your comfort zone. But hey, that's the fun in it! My grandmother and her pals went to a brunch show and had a blast. Not only will aerialists and dance performers dazzle you, you'll also get in a few good laughs too! Do be mindful that this is typically a 21 and up venue and tickets can be on the pricier side. If you do have guests under 21, call and speak with them about criteria and whether or not they will be allowed entry (i.e. if it's a special event). Brunch, dinner, and evening shows are all available for purchase depending on what you prefer.

SPORTS FANATICS

"Winning isn't everything, but wanting to win is."

– Vince Lombardi

29. BE A PART OF CARDINAL NATION

Missourians are serious about our baseball. And as the home of an 11 time World Series Championship winning team, we should be! Grab yourself some cracker jacks, a beer, and a Cardinal's jersey while at the massive Busch Stadium and witness why big names like Carpenter, Wainwright, Molina, and Wacha generate such buzz in the league. (Get there early though because parking can be a mad house!) And please, please, don't wear a Cubs t-shirt. You will get booed.

30. STANLEY CUP WINNING BLUES

Buy yourself a "We all Bleed Blue" jersey and head on over to the Enterprise Center in downtown St. Louis. While they've been in four of the cup finals, in 2019 the team finally took home the championship. Our team is proud and passionate, and so are the local fans. Not to mention the frequent ice fights and ground shaking glass slams, which will keep you on your toes in anticipation! Our team has had some of the most influential NHL players of all time wear the blue note, including Adam Oates, Wayne Gretzky, Brett Hull, and Martin Brodeur to name a few. After 16 Hall of Famers, it's easy to see why celebrities like Jon Hamm, Jenna Fischer, and Andy Cohen all back our Blues.

31. TAILGATE IN RED WITH THE KANSAS CITY CHIEFS

If you're visiting Kansas City, it'll be hard to walk down a street without seeing someone wearing a big, red Chief's jersey. This city loves their football team and it shows. Head over to Arrowhead Stadium early to beat traffic and be prepared as spaces are cash only and expensive. You can also stop into to the Ford Tail Gate District, which is free to enter and offers a number of game day activities.

32. WEAR SOME BOOTS AND HEAD TO THE RODEO

Along with an abundance of county fairs, Missouri hosts quite a few rodeos. I mean we are in the Midwest. Purchase a couple of tickets and watch as cowgirls barrel race with lightning speed and cowboys test their grip for a title. Maybe you'll even see some sheep herding dogs doing what they love with razor sharp focus! You can always find an MRCA show (Missouri Rodeo Cowboy Association) at our State Fair in August. So throw on a pair of boots, that old flannel, and enjoy the show.

MUSIC AND NIGHTLIFE

*"I'm afraid concerts spoil
people for everyday life."*

– L.M. Montgomery

33. HOLLYWOOD CASINO AMPHITHEATER

As far as outdoor venues go, this one is probably the most popular in Saint Louis. Summer shows are a staple for any local. You may see crowd surfing, stage diving, mosh pits, or the famed artist may just perform a show in the lawn area right in front of you! Seating with the roof of the stage overhead is closer and can be a bit more expensive but nice if you're trying to avoid inclement weather. The massive lawn that engulfs the surrounding scenery can host thousands of people but amazingly doesn't inhibit viewing. Massive live feed screens and speakers make you feel like you're right in front of the artist. Parking is ample so arrive whenever you feel like it. I do recommend eating beforehand, as food can be very expensive inside, as well as drinks. Bathrooms and

ATMS are ample as well. You'll find a few souvenir stands inside if you want to purchase a tee shirt to commemorate the experience!

34. ROCK OUT AT THE PAGEANT

Located within the historic Delmar Loop, this concert venue and nightlife hotspot hosts shows almost daily! Check their prohibited items list before your show to ensure you have a great time with minimum hold ups. Smoking, crowd surfing, and stage diving are also not acceptable inside the venue. It holds a bottom level where the stage is that lets you get up close and personal, as well as a balcony for awesome acoustics and to get a bird's eye venue of the whole scene. Arrive early to grab a close parking spot, spaces can be difficult to find. Plus there are tons of restaurants nearby so you can get your fill of amazing food before the show! I recommend Seoul Taco, Three Kings Public House, or Salt + Smoke.

35. RIDE A MECHANICAL BULL AT BALLPARK VILLAGE

This is the perfect place to go before game time or for an evening out. Ballpark Village is a massive space that boasts several top quality restaurants and bars within its walls. Try out your rodeo skills on a mechanical bull inside PBR St. Louis or dance the night away at the upscale Crown Room. You can take in a Cardinals win from one of the balconies that overlook our stadium or on one of the many massive viewing screens. Be mindful that parking can get quite pricey especially on game days; you may be best to use a ridesharing app in order to avoid the hassle and fees. Their website also has ample information on rates and availability if you prefer driving you or your family. If there is a special event they may charge a minimal cover fee for entry after certain hours.

Bonus St. Louis music venues that host amazing live music: Tin Roof, Blueberry Hill, Broadway Oyster Bar, and The Firebird.

SPRING AND SUMMER HITS

*"Summertime is always the best
of what might be."*

– Charles Bowden

36. SOAK UP THE SUN AT LAKE OF THE OZARKS

As a Midwestern state, Missourians get pretty excited about any big body of water within our state lines. Lake of the Ozarks is one of the most popular places for locals to visit in the summer months. Boat rentals are made readily available for all of your tubing, water skiing, or fishing needs. Lined with bars, restaurants, and the infamous "party cove" hangout spot, you'll likely leave with new pals, sunburns, and a serious hangover.

If you're looking for some activities off the water, check out Bridal Cave, Bagnell Dam, or one of the many manicured golf courses surrounding the area. Ha Ha Tonka State Park is also located here and has been voted one of the most beautiful spots in

Missouri. This gorgeous park is home to a natural bridge, hiking trails, historic castle ruins, and beautiful vantage of points of the Ozarks, bluffs, and pristine Ha Ha Tonka spring. Park hours change seasonally so please check their website for detailed information before your journey. Also be sure to check yourself for ticks during and after your state park visits, as they are common in Missouri. Wearing bug repellent, tucking your socks into your shoes, and carrying tweezers to remove them properly are always good precautions. Parking is available as are restrooms and a visitor's center.

37. BREAK A SWEAT AT TOWER GROVE PARK

Located next to the Missouri Botanical Garden and eclectic Tower Grove neighborhood, Tower Grove Park is a hub for local gatherings of all sorts. Most days of the week there will be some sort of free yoga / dance / running group or class that caters to various levels. Most of these are seasonal activities as its outdoors (check their Facebook page for more info). After you sweat it out, head over to Tropical Liqueurs and get a frozen alcohol infused slushy. Yum!

Bonus – Stop by Dunaway Books, within walking distance from the park. It's a great used local bookstore with heaps of inexpensive options to bring with you as you lounge in the grass under the trees. If you're feeling extra Missourian, buy a tale from famous local authors such as T.S. Eliot, Maya Angelou, Tennessee Williams, or Jonathan Franzen.

38. DIVERSITY ON ECCENTRIC CHEROKEE STREET

As your car pulls up to Cherokee Street, you'll see the postcard symbol of your arrival as a beautiful 20-foot tall sculpture of an indigenous man comes into view. This area located right next to downtown St. Louis is a well known for it's eccentric vibe and cultural diversity. Artists, antique hunters, beer lovers, and dancers will have their hands full. One of the most frequented events on Cherokee is their Cinco de Mayo celebration in May. You'll find people pouring into the streets adorned in bright colors and margaritas in hand for blocks.

39. STOP INTO OLD SAINT CHARLES

Looking for a local hot spot that combines the interests of history buffs, outdoor enthusiasts, and nightlife all in one? Look no further! Take a stroll down Main Street to see where Lewis and Clark rendezvoused. Bring the fishing poles and a blanket as you watch the Missouri River roll by (maybe you'll even catch a few huge Channel Catfish, our official state fish). Wear your new little black dress and dance the night away at Quintessential. Don't forget to stop into Picasso's for the most popular coffee joint in town. On Thursday's they also host open-mic nights for those more musically inclined!

Close to Main Street you will also find heaps of exciting and popular attractions near by. I recommend heading up the road to Adrenaline Zone for a few rounds of demolition ball and laser tag with the family. Or head over to the dazzling Ameristar Casino where you'll find a spa, hotel, restaurants, bars, and dancing.

FALL AND WINTER ADVENTURES

"I prefer winter and fall, when you feel the bone structure of the landscape. Something waits beneath it; the whole story doesn't show."

– Andrew Wyeth

40. GET SPOOKED AT ONE OF OUR FAMOUS HAUNTED HOUSES

If you're lucky enough to be exploring Missouri in the month of October, we've got some spook-tacular treats in store for you! This state LOVES our Halloween season and there is never a shortage of scary sights to take in. Some of the top-ranked haunted houses in the USA are located here, including The Darkness and Lemp Mansion. (Seriously, I broke my big toe running into a wall because I was so scared a few years back)

Bonus - The Lemp Mansion is expanded into a home of ghost tours, a restaurant, and an Inn. For those seeking creepy thrills, this is the spot for you. You can attend mystery dinners, annual events, or host private parties for special occasions. Ghost tours are extremely popular at Lemp and should be booked in advance (they can get a bit pricey as well). At the end of your tour your host may even attempt psychic communication with the spirits!

41. ICE STATING AT STEINBERG RINK

A St. Louis winter just isn't complete without a trip to the infamous Steinberg Rink! Located in Forest Park, skates are available for rental inside and it has become a family favorite for locals. Look up at the dazzling lights and decorations strung across the rink from above. Get in a snowball fight with the kids or show them your skillful snowman crafting abilities. Sip hot cocoa next to the outdoor fire pits for a cozy evening out. And wear some thick socks because those ice skate blisters can hurt!

The ice rink is usually open from mid November until late February. It is cash only but ATMs are available on site if you'd like to use them. Your ticket will get you admission into the rink all day long.

42. SPEND THE DAY AT DELMAR LOOP

Fondly known as "The Loop" this curated collection of delicious food, storefronts, and entertainment is a staple in St. Louis. Stop into Vintage Vinyl and pick out a favorite record from decades past. Take a selfie with the infamous Chuck Berry Statue. Indulge your sweet tooth with one of the most decadent root beer floats you've ever seen. Giggle and gawk at the stylish second hand finds inside Avalon Exchange. The list of unique places to explore here can get long winded, but aside from the previously mentioned, we can't leave out Blueberry Hill, the Tivoli Theater, Pin-Up Bowl, and Salt & Smoke. This avenue has even been voted as one of the best streets in the United States, come see why! Bonus: if you're looking for a place to stay nearby, the Moonrise Hotel is within the loop and includes a stunning and popular rooftop terrace bar.

While you're visiting don't forget about the Loop Ice Carnival! Winter traveling can be difficult, especially if you're not one to leap on a pair of snow skis or shred slopes on a snowboard (if this IS more your style check out Hidden Valley Ski Resort). The Loop Ice Carnival offers an opportunity for St. Louis city locals to stretch their legs during the cold winter and have some fun with activities for all ages. This themed weekend event has a ball, carnival rides, ice sculptures, scavenger hunts, and more. Typically the event is held in mid January and to gain entry they request a small donation or canned good.

GETTING AROUND AND STAYING SAFE

"The road makes a noise all its own. It's a single note that stretches in all directions, low and nearly inaudible, only I could hear it loud and persistent."

– Gregory Galloway

43. SHOULD I RENT A CAR?

The MetroLink and MetroBus are available for public transit in Saint Louis. Visit their Metro Transit website for a list of stops and schedules or to buy a pass online. One day all-inclusive adventure passes are available online for cheap, as are pricier one month passes. Be careful, as many MetroLink stops and bus stops can become dangerous in the evenings with a large homeless population in the city. Bus systems mainly serve within the county, which work well for those wanting to stay within city limits. The MetroLink light rail expands about 50 miles outside of the city and into parts of our neighboring state,

Illinois. However, Missouri is a very large state and with many exciting places to explore outside of the city limits, I recommend renting a car. The freedom and safety it will give you is unmatched, and renting is made easily available at Lambert Airport. Uber and Lyft are also very common especially in bigger cities such as St. Louis, Kansas City, and Springfield.

44. AREAS TO AVOID IN SAINT LOUIS

As with every city, there are dangers to be aware of and avoid. Saint Louis is not immune to this fact and it's extremely important to be aware of certain streets and neighborhoods that are prone to crime. North Saint Louis and East St. Louis are some key areas that can experience higher volumes in criminal activity. Kingshighway, Natural Bridge, Wells-Goodfellow, Baden, Cardonelet, and Hyde Park are all areas I would recommend avoiding to ensure a safe trip as they tend to have higher crime rates and risks. When booking a place to stay for your visit, your best bet will always be to look west of the city as it gets much safer the further west you go. No matter where you are, always be vigilant at night and stay aware of your surroundings.

DRINKS THAT IMPRESS

"Without question the greatest invention in the history of mankind is beer. Oh, I grant you that the wheel was also a fine invention but the wheel does not go nearly as well with pizza."

- Dave Barry

45. SNAG A TOUR AT ANHEUSER-BUSCH BREWERY

St. Louis city is home to one of the largest beer conglomerates in the nation. Luckily, visiting the home of names such as Budweiser, Michelob Ultra, and Bud Light is relatively cheap! Download the app and book yourself a brewery experience that will be unforgettable. Some packages include photo opportunities with our infamous Anheuser Clydesdales. The brewery also features a beautiful Biergarten that host's monthly beer & food pairing dinner events. If you're in town over the winter holiday, stop in and witness the magic of the annual

Brewery Lights. This event is free and family friendly!

46. SIP THROUGH THE WINE TRAIL OF HERMANN, MO

Welcome to the Tuscany of Missouri! Hermann wineries are infamous for their delicious blends and unique history. Stone Hill Winery and Adam Puchta Winery are among some of the favorites. (Fun fact- the Adam Puchta Winery is actually the oldest family run winery in North America!) Hermann boasts a top quality and hand picked Wine Trail, which can be followed via trolley (trolley tickets are fairly cheap) and takes you to seven family owned wineries with outstanding reputations. More information on tasting room etiquette and trail tickets can be found online for purchase. Seasonal wine & food pairing weekend events can also be booked. Remember you must be 21+ to participate!

If you're interested in checking out some stops outside of the winery wheelhouse, fear not! There are plenty of options available for food, shopping, or history. Stop into favorites such as the Hermann

Wurst Haus, Black Walnut Bistro, or Espresso Laine for delicious food and drinks. History buffs can get their fill at Deutscheim State Historic Site or Hermann Farm. Visitors looking to purchase unique souvenirs should stop into Hermann's Attic & Antique Mall or Type Styles.

ART AND ARCHITECTURE BUFFS

"Art enables us to find ourselves and lose ourselves at the same time."

– Thomas Merton

47. SAINT LOUIS ART MUSEUM

Art aficionados unite! From Van Gogh to Edmonia Lewis, Artemisia Gentileschi to the mummy of Amun's priest, St. Louis Art Museum is worth an afternoon of admiration. Themed installations are regularly updated for special events so check out the website before you arrive if you are keen on seeing a specific artist's work. Did I mention they have free entry and free marking? This place is a bargain!

Bonus – the museum is located within Forest Park, the most popular park in Saint Louis city. If you have time, stop into The Jewel Box (a beautiful greenhouse inside the park that was recently renovated) for some pictures. Or take a stroll to the local boathouse restaurant afterwards and rent a paddleboat for extra fun and gorgeous views of art hill. (If you're visiting in winter you may see kiddos with their sleds gliding down this infamous hill. It's a favorite sledding spot for locals!)

48. SNAP UNIQUE PICTURES AT THE GRAFFITI WALL

Attention to those with an affliction for street art, this is your spot! Bring your camera and a sweet outfit for some trip pictures that will make your friends gawk. Also fondly named The Mural Mile, the Graffiti Wall Saint Louis is a collection of creative expression from over 200 local artists. It'll give you a great sense of city culture and maybe even leave you feeling inspired to create a masterpiece of your own!

Do be mindful that some areas of the city can be dangerous, so I would recommend bringing someone with you and come here during the day, not night. However this is a popular spot amount many locals and tourists to take photos so don't worry about being the only visitors. The wall is located along the riverfront in an abandoned industrial area, great for people that enjoy exploring off the beaten path!

49. VICTORIAN STYLE HOMES OF LAFAYETTE SQUARE

Downtown Saint Louis is bustling with neighborhood gems if you know the right places to look. Lafayette Square is no exception! Park your car and take your time enjoying the historical and colorful homes and buildings that this center is known for. Stop by Lafayette Park to catch a glimpse of the graceful swans that call it home. House tours are available for the history buffs that want to learn more about the Victorian Era architecture ling the streets.

Bailey's Chocolate Bar is a local favorite, with decadent alcohol infused and non-alcoholic dessert creations that aim to impress. Early birds can enjoy stretching it out during an AM session at Southtown Yoga. Afterwards stop into Four Muddy Paws and grab a delicious treat to bring home for your furry family member. Festivals and special events are common at Lafayette Square so check out their calendar for a list of dates!

50. RIDE UP THE FAMOUS ARCH

No trip to Missouri is complete without visiting the arch. Fondly referred to as "The Gateway to the Midwest", the arch is a staple of this state, and the city of St. Louis. It's centrally located downtown and close to many popular city attractions. The arch often offers rides to the top, giving visitors the opportunity to get amazing photos overlooking the entire cityscape. (It's also a popular field trip for local kids – my 5th grade had a blast here!) Feel your ears pop and your adrenaline rush as you gain 630 feet in under 5 minutes in the tramway. If you want to save a few bucks and some time waiting in line, visit the Gateway Arch on a weekday instead of a weekend. Snap a few selfies and if you have time check out the free museum to learn more about the history of how this architectural beauty was made.

Fun Fact: The Arch is such an iconic piece of architecture that it's made cameos in movies and TV shows for decades. Some of the most well known include movies such as "National Lampoon's Vacation", "Up in the Air", and the TV show "Defiance".

TOP REASONS TO BOOK THIS TRIP

Music: Missouri has an abundance of venues and local bands playing every night of the week. You'll always have the opportunity to dance the night away or soak up the ambiance of a collection of genres.

Food: The food is amazing. Barbeque, toasted raviolis, pizza, Italian, and ice cream are constantly being transformed into delicious, creative dishes that aim to please.

Festivals: No matter where you are in Missouri or what time of year you are visiting, I will guarantee you that a festival is being thrown. We love hosting events to celebrate our diversity, passions, and make memories with loved ones.

PACKING AND PLANNING TIPS

A Week before Leaving

- Arrange for someone to take care of pets and water plants.

- Email and Print important Documents.

- Get Visa and vaccines if needed.

- Check for travel warnings.

- Stop mail and newspaper.

- Notify Credit Card companies where you are going.

- Passports and photo identification is up to date.

- Pay bills.

- Copy important items and download travel Apps.

- Start collecting small bills for tips.

- Have post office hold mail while you are away.

- Check weather for the week.

- Car inspected, oil is changed, and tires have the correct pressure.

- Check airline luggage restrictions.

- Download Apps needed for your trip.

Right Before Leaving

- Contact bank and credit cards to tell them your location.

- Clean out refrigerator.

- Empty garbage cans.

- Lock windows.

- Make sure you have the proper identification with you.

- Bring cash for tips.

- Remember travel documents.

- Lock door behind you.

- Remember wallet.

- Unplug items in house and pack chargers.

- Change your thermostat settings.

- Charge electronics, and prepare camera memory cards.

READ OTHER
GREATER THAN A TOURIST
BOOKS

Greater Than a Tourist- Geneva Switzerland: 50 Travel Tips from a Local by Amalia Kartika

Greater Than a Tourist- St. Croix US Birgin Islands USA: 50 Travel Tips from a Local by Tracy Birdsall

Greater Than a Tourist- San Juan Puerto Rico: 50 Travel Tips from a Local by Melissa Tait

Greater Than a Tourist – Lake George Area New York USA: 50 Travel Tips from a Local by Janine Hirschklau

Greater Than a Tourist – Monterey California United States: 50 Travel Tips from a Local by Katie Begley

Greater Than a Tourist – Chanai Crete Greece: 50 Travel Tips from a Local by Dimitra Papagrigoraki

Greater Than a Tourist – The Garden Route Western Cape Province South Africa: 50 Travel Tips from a Local by Li-Anne McGregor van Aardt

Greater Than a Tourist – Sevilla Andalusia Spain: 50 Travel Tips from a Local by Gabi Gazon

Children's Book: *Charlie the Cavalier Travels the World* by Lisa Rusczyk Ed. D.

> TOURIST

Follow us on Instagram for beautiful travel images:
http://Instagram.com/GreaterThanATourist

Follow *Greater Than a Tourist* on Amazon.
>Tourist Podcast
>T Website
>T Youtube
>T Facebook
>T TikTok
>T Goodreads
>T Amazon
>T Mailing List
>T Pinterest
>T Instagram
>T Twitter
>T SoundCloud
>T LinkedIn
>T Map

> TOURIST

At *Greater Than a Tourist*, we love to share travel tips with you. How did we do? What guidance do you have for how we can give you better advice for your next trip? Please send your feedback to GreaterThanaTourist@gmail.com as we continue to improve the series. We appreciate your constructive feedback. Thank you.

METRIC CONVERSIONS

TEMPERATURE

110° F — — 40° C
100° F —
90° F — — 30° C
80° F —
70° F — — 20° C
60° F —
50° F — — 10° C
40° F —
32° F — — 0° C
20° F —
10° F — — -10° C
0° F — — -18° C
-10° F —
-20° F — — -30° C

To convert F to C:

Subtract 32, and then multiply by 5/9 or .5555.

To Convert C to F:

Multiply by 1.8 and then add 32.

32F = 0C

LIQUID VOLUME

To Convert:...................Multiply by
U.S. Gallons to Liters................ 3.8
U.S. Liters to Gallons 26
Imperial Gallons to U.S. Gallons 1.2
Imperial Gallons to Liters....... 4.55
Liters to Imperial Gallons 22
1 Liter = .26 U.S. Gallon
1 U.S. Gallon = 3.8 Liters

DISTANCE

To convert ....Multiply by
Inches to Centimeters 2.54
Centimeters to Inches 39
Feet to Meters........................ .3
Meters to Feet 3.28
Yards to Meters 91
Meters to Yards 1.09
Miles to Kilometers 1.61
Kilometers to Miles............ .62
1 Mile = 1.6 km
1 km = .62 Miles

WEIGHT

1 Ounce = .28 Grams
1 Pound = .4555 Kilograms
1 Gram = .04 Ounce
1 Kilogram = 2.2 Pounds

TRAVEL QUESTIONS

- Do you bring presents home to family or friends after a vacation?

- Do you get motion sick?

- Do you have a favorite billboard?

- Do you know what to do if there is a flat tire?

- Do you like a sun roof open?

- Do you like to eat in the car?

- Do you like to wear sun glasses in the car?

- Do you like toppings on your ice cream?

- Do you use public bathrooms?

- Did you bring a cell phone and does it have power?

- Do you have a form of identification with you?

- Have you ever been pulled over by a cop?

- Have you ever given money to a stranger on a road trip?

- Have you ever taken a road trip with animals?

- Have you ever gone on a vacation alone?

- Have you ever run out of gas?

- If you could move to any place in the world, where would it be?

- If you could travel anywhere in the world, where would you travel?

- If you could travel in any vehicle, which one would it be?

- If you had three things to wish for from a magic genie, what would they be?

- If you have a driver's license, how many times did it take you to pass the test?

- What are you the most afraid of on vacation?

- What do you want to get away from the most when you are on vacation?

- What foods smell bad to you?

- What item do you bring on ever trip with you away from home?

- What makes you sleepy?

- What song would you love to hear on the radio when you're cruising on the highway?

- What travel job would you want the least?

- What will you miss most while you are away from home?

- What is something you always wanted to try?

- What is the best road side attraction that you ever saw?

- What is the farthest distance you ever biked?

- What is the farthest distance you ever walked?

- What is the weirdest thing you needed to buy while on vacation?

- What is your favorite candy?

- What is your favorite color car?

- What is your favorite family vacation?

- What is your favorite food?

- What is your favorite gas station drink or food?

- What is your favorite license plate design?

- What is your favorite restaurant?

- What is your favorite smell?

- What is your favorite song?

- What is your favorite sound that nature makes?

- What is your favorite thing to bring home from a vacation?

- What is your favorite vacation with friends?

- What is your favorite way to relax?

- Where is the farthest place you ever traveled in a car?

- Where is the farthest place you ever went North, South, East and West?

- Where is your favorite place in the world?

- Who is your favorite singer?

- Who taught you how to drive?

- Who will you miss the most while you are away?

- Who if the first person you will contact when you get to your destination?

- Who brought you on your first vacation?

- Who likes to travel the most in your life?

- Would you rather be hot or cold?

- Would you rather drive above, below, or at the speed limited?

- Would you rather drive on a highway or a back road?

- Would you rather go on a train or a boat?

- Would you rather go to the beach or the woods?

TRAVEL BUCKET LIST

1.

2.

3.

4.

5.

6.

7.

8.

9.

10.

NOTES